How to improve the work environment

Ricardo Pérez P.

Copyright reserved

Chapter 1 - What is the work environment

- Concept and Structure
- Influence factors of in the labor climate
- Negatives and Positives
- Communication, Collaboration, Leadership
- Interests ambiguity

Chapter 2 - Organizational Culture

- Organizational Culture Concepts
- Structure and organization
- Congruence
- Business mission, Business vision, Philosophy, Values
- The manager
- What does a director look for in an employee
- Recommendations for managers in favor of a positive work environment
- The employee
- What is a employee looking for in a company
- Recommendations for employees in favor of a positive work environment

Chapter 3 - Profound changes

Chapter 4 - Change strategies and improvement

- Recruitment and staff selection
- Polls
- Dynamics
- Effectiveness
- Reinforcement cycles
- Recognize and congratulate
- Work policies

Chapter 5 - Indicators of change measurement

Let's start with the first steps to get you started making changes today:

First we must be clear about what the working environment and its structure is, to identify opportunity areas of and weaknesses, to know where to begin to solve problems that prevent us from enjoying a positive working environment.

Everything that happens in a workplace, with people who interact to do their individual or team work, influences the work environment, I mention some of the most common that can destabilize a company internally:

- Bad communication
- Disrespect
- Lack of training
- Lack of the right tools
- Lack of motivation and recognition
- Don't listen to the employees
- Do not involve them in the company's problems
- A boss without leadership and arrogant
- An uncompromising directive

Do you identify with any of these points? Don't worry, after reading this book, you will have found the solution.

The work climate is a very important factor that in a positive sense maintains a sustained development of the company and productivity, but the great dilemma of employers today is how to combine development, productivity and a good work climate at the same time, the Answer is very simple, I would summarize it in 3 simple words: empathy, synergy and leadership.

If a company makes everyone work based on these concepts, a powerful combination of attitudes and actions will be achieved in an environment of harmony so extraordinary that a positive work climate will be generated.

The work environment is a vital part of an organization, it is what improves productivity and stability, without these elements, there is simply no growth.

Chapter 1

What is the work environment?

Concept

Let's see it as a mixture of thoughts, attitudes and customs trapped between four walls that move in all directions and when they are on the same path, but in opposite directions, collide and a conflict is generated that affects relationships and workplace harmony.

But why not make it go in the same direction, producing a positive momentum of communication and respect?

It is achieved by creating a bilateral force with an influence that results in a working relationship based on the main pillars mentioned above between managers and workers.

But it is important to understand that, the work environment begins to be built from the very conception of a business idea, from when the philosophy of the company is defined, not when there is already a conflict to remedy as it normally happens.

It is normal for companies to worry about improving the work environment when they already have a very advanced problem, using climate surveys with which they will never be able to know for certain the true situation, much less the real feeling of the employees.

This bilateral force is a form of contact that is generated by 2 sources and from 4 main points:

- From manager to manager
- From manager to employee
- From employee to manager
- From employee to employee

The way in which this contact occurs will be the type of work environment that will affect daily coexistence, whether positive or negative.

For that reason, communication is one of the most determining factors in creating stronger relationships of trust among staff at all levels.

Making group dynamics, helps a lot to improve communication and integration, among all staff at all levels.

Positive inertia refers to the influence caused by a positive behavior of a person who is contagious towards others, but who does so out of self-conviction with all of them.

"Example will always influence more than words."

You must ensure that each employee understands that this is a will agreement, in which everyone must participate regardless of their job position, because everyone equally suffers or enjoys every day, but that depends on what each one contributes.

C ada employee is responsible for his own behavior, not only respecting the rules or policies, also with the conviction to implement the values and the values of the company.

We must start by generating change in ourselves before trying to bring about change in others, and so on until we create positive inertia that generates general change.

• Create a good work environment first, it will be more productive.

• Wanting more productivity first, you will get less productivity and a bad work environment.

"We cannot demand from others what we ourselves are not capable of giving."

Structure

The work environment is supported by four main pillars and each one has a very important function, since it is based on human behavior; if one is missing, you will lose your balance and there will be difficulties, which are so common today.

WORK ENVIRONMENT			
TRUST	COMMUNICATION	DISCIPLINE	RESPECT

Trust:

For the work to be done, it is necessary to trust our work team, our colleagues, our superiors and especially ourselves.

Trust is having the certainty that your own work is backed by that of others, that there is harmony, there is no professional jealousy or envy, everyone helps each other and if something goes wrong, no one wastes time looking for culprits, everyone seeks solutions To continue, everyone supports each other and everyone works to achieve the same goal.

Trust is not asked for; first it is offered, then it is won and in the end it is shared.

Communication:

In the way we use it, it will be the effect it will cause, that is, encourage, congratulate, never recriminate, offend or humiliate.

Proper communication between two or more people is the only way that we must make ourselves understood, therefore, we must always make sure that our words have an intention and a positive effect, the way of expressing ourselves, is also the image that we project, always communicate clearly, concisely and with respect.

Discipline:

It is the way to require ourselves to do what we have to do, when we have to do it and the way we have to do it, discipline is a habit that generates highly effective people to work, they are also the ones who start to cause a change in themselves before wanting to influence others to change, they are used to being the example to follow.

Let's make discipline a habit in all areas of our lives and we will see the results soon, but it has to be out of conviction, not out of obligation.

Respect:

In my opinion, it is the most important of all, respect strengthens trust and interpersonal relationships, it is the element of greatest influence in a favorable or unfavorable work environment, although we know that it is difficult to get a person to change their habits.

Good recruitment and selection of people who work in our company is important, because if they show that they respect as a way of life, we can be sure that they will be a negative future leader that will probably contaminate others with bad attitudes.

Respect in a workplace, can be with some of these examples or all

- Express ideas, not impose them.
- Respect the ideas of others and reach agreements.
- Do not criticize, understand and advise.
- Do not make fun of or humiliate people.
- Respect people, regardless of their level or position, gender, religion or sexual preference.
- Respect the rules.
- Accept mistakes, rather than blame.
- Respect what is not yours.
- Use the company's resources correctly.
- Respect hierarchies, without limiting communication.
- If you are a boss, do not abuse your authority, use it to help.

It is necessary to strive to have upright people with most of these qualities as collaborators, to have a group of highly mentally and emotionally capable people, to generate a positive work climate and to be able to create a solid and successful company.

Factors that influence the work environment

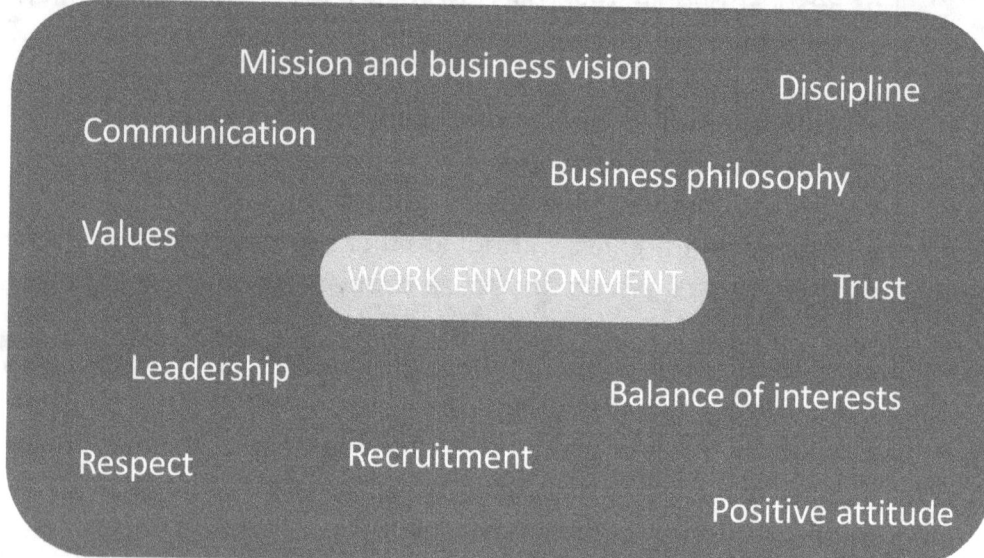

Analyze these factors and reflect if you have paid attention to all of them and if they are working well, if not, then we will be able to identify which problem or problems you will need to address and resolve with your employees.

Negative factors

Common differences

Some or all of these differences can be found in any company, if it is not given importance, it can create a negative work climate.

Money and work

- The employee wants to earn more and work less
- The manager wants to pay less and make them work more

Result = negative work climate because the employee shows little awareness and does not value his work, in the same way, the manager shows little awareness and makes his employees overwork and has little respect for them.

Suggestions:

For the employee: Having a job is a privilege, it is a way to grow every day as a person and as a professional, it is an opportunity to develop skills and learn new things, but he must also be aware that the company strives to pay him a fair salary, and strive to work with efficiency and quality.

For the manager: employees are not machines, they are people who need to work to earn an income, but they need a balance in their work and personal life, because that balance will give them the possibility of being more productive in the agreed time, without having than taking time out of your personal life. With that balance, they will also be able to do their job with the expected quality, without the need to pressure or threaten them.

Time and work

- The employee wants time to work and time for his personal life.
- The manager wants less time for his living people and more time to work.

Result = negative work climate because the employee does not feel understood and with a feeling of frustration, for not being able to rest or spend time in his personal life after work, and cannot have a mental and emotional balance to perform his job better and with motivation.

Suggestion

Create flexible hours and find a balance between work hours and hours of rest, so that they do not affect productivity, but neither the personal life of the employee.

Training and work

- The employee wants support to learn and develop to do his job better.
- The manager wants the employee to learn how he can

Result = frustration feeling because the employee does not feel supported, anxiety because more quality is required in their work without the support of training.

Suggestion

Create a specialized training program with indicators of impact on work and personal growth, the training of employees will always cause a double benefit, for the employee in his personal development and for the company in having more efficient and productive employees.

Recognition and work

- The employee expects recognition and encouragement to work motivated and committed to improve their performance.
- The manager believes that it is an obligation of the employee to do his job well because that is what he is paid for.

Result = the employee feels unmotivated. Recognition is a need that encourages us to continue with the same commitment, without recognition, the impulse loses strength until it disappears and gradually diminishes the motivation.

Suggestion

Create strategies to encourage employees to compete in a positive way. Organize events between departments or individually, but it is very important to create many possibilities to win because that will motivate employees more than when there are few opportunities, feeling the employee that has little chance of winning and will not feel very motivated to compete.

Common differences prevail in most companies, because interests go in the opposite direction and neither side is willing to budge, the key is to get them to go in the same direction to create positive inertia.

One way to do this is to find a balance in which each one gives up a little in their interests, and to know that the positive inertia that will be generated will go in the same direction.

This means more growth, higher income, but most importantly, you succeed in changing negatively to the positive work environment.

Arrogance at work

The work environment in a company is a matter of acting with values, with maturity and respect for our collaborators, regardless of the level, because the level is only to define who has greater responsibility in decision-making, and not to determine the value If one person is superior to another, the value of a person is measured first by his integrity and then by what he does to the development and success of the company.

In all companies, there are managers who misuse power, because they use it to fuel their arrogance, instead of using power to help, to contribute, because power is finally the possibility for a boss to decide, create, analyze, judge and to change something.

Unfortunately, there are few managers who use power to serve, if we could change the concept of the use of that power to all the people in a company, we would achieve a significant transformation in the work environment of companies and they will work as teams with willing people and less arrogant people.

Everyone in a company is just as important at any level, and if everyone in the organization understands it, a positive attitude will spread and infect everyone.

Positive factors:

Attitude

A positive attitude is an essential element that generates a favorable working environment for the achievement of objectives and a constant growth of the staff and the organization.

The positive attitude is made up of several aspects, which are based on the relationship between managers and employees, hence the importance of creating effective and simple communication systems based on trust and mutual respect.

In a collective attitude, it cannot trigger anything other than a totally favorable work environment.

To better understand the concept, let's look at these comparative examples:

Negative attitude:

1. The CEO of a company calls his Area Director for scolding him because he did not make the right decision.
2. The Area Director calls his Manager and scolds him for not giving him the correct information.
3. The manager scolds his coordinator because he did not review the information before delivering it
4. The coordinator scolds his assistant because he did not work well.

Negative result:

- Frustration feeling
- Mistrust. And each doubts his own ability, more mistakes will be made.
- There is no will to recognize mistakes and resolve them.
- No goal achievement.
- Misuse of power in a position to blame, not resolve.
- Bad work environment between employees and managers that generates resentment, mistrust, low motivation.
- The problem was not corrected.

Analysis of the negative result and conclusion:

- Each released his frustration on his immediate subordinate.
- No one was responsible for what they did wrong
- They just wanted to break free from guilt

In a company that works as a team, therefore, the bad work done is badly done by everyone involved, each one according to his role, but in the end everyone is responsible.

Everyone had a negative reaction, no one provided a solution to the problem, everyone evaded it.

- No one recognized that they did something wrong

Positive attitude:

1. The General Director of a company calls his Area Director to **ask him** why he did not make the right decision, together they analyze the problem, detect the error and find the solution.
2. The Area Director calls his Manager and **asks** him why he did not give him the correct information, together they analyze the problem, detect the error and find a solution.
3. The Manager **asks** his Coordinator why he did not review the information before delivering it, together they analyze the problem, detect the error and find a solution
4. El Coordinator **asks** his assistant because it did not work well together analyze the problem, they detected the error and find a solution.

Positive result:

- Feeling of satisfaction for correcting a team problem.
- Feeling of confidence and nobody doubts their own ability, the mistake will hardly be repeated.
- There is no ego attitude and there is a wide willingness to recognize the error and solve it
- The goal is achieved.
- The power of a position was used to help and solve, not to evade.
- Healthier work environment, without resentment, there is motivation to improve and there is also a feeling of commitment, which is what managers expect from their employees.
- The problem was corrected regardless of what level the problem was generated at.

Analysis of the positive result:

- Each one assumed his role as coach leader
- Each acknowledged his mistake and had the willingness to find ways to correct

There was a big change in attitude

- Scolding was replaced by solutions
- There were no culprits
- A tense situation was not created that resulted in a bad work environment
- Each one grew professionally and humanely
- With greater confidence in themselves and among their peers.

Communication

Communication in a company must have as a priority to guarantee that all people have the same information to work, it is generated by the need to specify an idea that must be shared so that each employee knows what their responsibility is. until the idea is understood.

It sounds easy, but it is not. Let's start by identifying the two aspects of communication that are generated in a workplace and between many people at the same time and also sequentially.

The first aspect refers to the communication of a boss to indicate the activities to his team, the communication must be clear and concise, in times, forms, to solve doubts and everything necessary to carry out the tasks without problems.

In these cases it is very important that those responsible for planning and coordinating tasks maintain an attitude of solving any doubts or problems that may arise from their subordinates.

Just as subordinates themselves must maintain an attitude of readiness to find out and resolve their own doubts and minimize errors that may cause difficulties or damage relationships between coworkers causing a negative work climate.

The boss must keep in mind at all times that his job is not just about delegating, the job of a boss must be that of a leader who plans and organizes his team, he is the first to start executing tasks so that his collaborators follow their example, that is also a very effective way of communicating without words.

Communication in a company can be: in person, in print, by phone and electronically, but in all of them it must be respectful to cause the positive effect.

The second aspect refers to the freedom and confidence of workers to communicate openly with their colleagues and superiors, on personal and work matters.

But that trust implies not being afraid to express your opinions about everything that happens in the workplace, suggestions, warnings, acknowledgments, constructive criticism, advice and everything that helps maintain favorable communication between all workers at all levels. hierarchical.

All with the same conviction to use communication as another tool to maintain a favorable work environment.

All with the same conviction of using communication as another tool to maintain a favorable work environment.

The positive attitude in communication is an essential element to generate a favorable work environment for the achievement of objectives, a constant growth of the staff and of the organization in general.

"Communication with respect is the shortest route to building ideal harmony in the workplace."

Collaboration

Teamwork

One of the most important aspects of achieving a positive work environment, collaboration means working together in harmony, but the key to achieving it properly is:

Know the weaknesses and strengths, talents and limitations, likes and dislikes of our colleagues to complement each other, that is, find a way to adapt to each other in the work teams to be able to collaborate all together and create such solidity, allowing fluidity in the processes and smartly achieving goals in an environment of people willing to work as a team, rather than divide.

Collaboration also consists of having the initiative to help those who need it for the pleasure of doing it and feel satisfaction when doing it.

Leadership

Leadership is a skill that unfortunately not all people can develop because it depends on having some characteristics such as:

- Service attitude
- Emotional intelligence
- Empathy
- Desires for improvement
- Wide willingness to support others.
- Self-confidence
- Great ability to convey enthusiasm.
- Motivator by example, not with authority.

If we manage to develop these skills in our leaders, we will have leaders who will lead their work team to achieve objectives and develop their team by exploiting all their abilities and, most importantly, it will be an important of change agent.

Personal development should be a joint effort between the leaders and the Training and Development area.

The job descriptions and profiles required by the company, especially in key positions where people with extensive leadership skills are required, must be fully attached to the company values and philosophy, this will greatly help to count among the team of leaders with people with a positive attitude that generates a good work environment.

A true leader, he forgets to be just a boss and tries to form new leaders, to grow all together.

Personal development and leadership is done with these three factors mainly:

• Gain knowledge and experience.
• Skill development
• Enrichment of culture

Fulfilling these factors, the personal and professional growth of employees is truly achieved, but unfortunately, it is very common in companies the belief that, if the boss helps his team to develop their skills, they will increase their chances of achieving the same level as him and then the boss will think that he can lose his position and that someone from his team can get it.

Thinking in this way seriously damages the company's growth potential, because it slows down the development of personnel at all levels, and few managers recognize the need to encourage their leaders to continue preparing.

Leaders who do not think this way teach, but do not keep what they know, they transmit it and acquire new knowledge and skills with which they maintain constant growth, but each one with the bases they already have, the great challenge for leaders is never to stop their growth so as not to be overtaken by their subordinates, this competition generates constantly growing people.

Training courses seem to be the only way that companies consider for the growth of workers, but it will never be enough for the acquisition of knowledge, since managers must ensure that their leaders are aware of their duty as true leaders to transmit knowledge of everyday during work.

In the development of personnel skills, the participation of the organization's leaders is necessary to achieve sustained growth, because the development of skills in real and everyday situations of daily work is a very effective way of learning and that is not obtained for attending training courses.

Although in this case, we have the same problem as leaders of not participating in the development of skills of their subordinates and it is necessary to make them aware that this is the only way to generate true skill development, to better perform the job.

Interest difference

One of the great secrets about how to start building a positive work environment is that the interests of the workers and those of the company are as closely related as possible.

Analyzing the interests of the workers and the company helps to identify the adjustments that need to be made, to reduce the difference in interests, to generate a positive work climate and keep it that way for a long time.

Identify the interests of your employees, the profiles you are looking for in the new elements and the interests of your company.

To the extent that mutual interests are tied, a great step will have been taken towards building an ideal work environment.

Many employers think that the most important thing for the company must be the interests of the company before those of the employees, the most intelligent thing is to seek, as everything in life, a balance of interests between

the employer and its employees , to create a true sense of commitment and not only the obligation to do the job without any motivation.

Chapter 2

Organizational culture

Organizational Culture Concepts

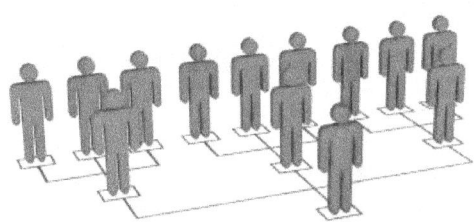

Organizational Culture can be understood from several angles, but in a simple explanation, we could say that:

It is to achieve the fusion of ideas and attitudes that generate a harmonious way of working together, following all the same rules, to play the game of organized work.

To achieve this merger, we can start from three elements, and from there continue to expand our vision, and be able to understand how to create an organizational culture that allows us to build a work environment based on ideal work climate and productivity, to achieve objectives and drive growth, and As the organizational culture of the company is enriched, add all the other elements that are necessary to achieve it.

Shared success

It is the way in which a manager, once they have achieved the expected success, is grateful and recognizes the effort of all the people who worked with him, sacrificed with him and believed in his ideas.

You can be thankful in many ways, not only with a financial reward, they can be trips, gifts, rest days, financial support for studies, etc.

It is also how a coworker recognizes and congratulates another coworker on their success, rather than envy.

As an example, let's do a simple exercise by answering yourself the following questions:

As an example, let's do a simple exercise by answering yourself the following questions:

How many times have you sincerely congratulated a coworker or how many times do you remember seeing a colleague recognize and congratulate another colleague or boss, or manager, sincerely and spontaneously for any achievement whatsoever, or simply for do your job well?.

It is easier to criticize or feel envy for those who achieve something, to change those attitudes, in addition to contributing directly to generating a good work climate, it also helps the positive organizational culture of the company.

Mutual respect

Mutual respect is a value that helps people interact in an appropriate way, because without respect, there is simply nothing, there is no trust, no good communication and there is no commitment of any worker, respect strengthens human relationships, gives the possibility of being better people and being able to achieve our personal goals and those of the company.

But that respect has to be in both directions, because if it is only in one direction, at some point it will break and there will be difficulties that will impact the work environment.

To start creating an ideal organizational culture with a stronger foundation, managers must start by feeling and treating all their workers with respect from the lowest level to the highest level, all deserve treatment with respect, a sincere greeting and friendly, we all have the same value as people.

Workers must also feel and treat their managers with respect, mutual respect is the tolerance with which they coexist daily among a group of people with many differences between them and everything influences the working environment during a work day.

Support at work

It means being able to trust our coworkers so that each one from their roles and responsibilities enhances and values the work of others, this is teamwork with all its potential, it is to create harmony and a sense of shared responsibility and not just one same, so that the work flows and the objectives are reached.

Organizational Culture and its strengths

An organizational culture is deficient, when in a company it has not been possible to mold the two parts of which it is made up:

Culture:
Ideas, customs, beliefs, knowledge, experiences, habits, etc.

Organization:
People with different cultures, carrying out activities working in harmony and synchronized in times and ways to achieve the same goal.

The great challenge then is to find a way to mold them in such a way that the organization is stronger than the culture, until an agreement of wills and a synchronization of emotions are achieved.

What needs to be done to shape a positive organizational culture?

Leadership:

It is very important for an ideal organizational culture, they are the drivers of the development and growth of companies, without positive leaders there is no motivation, there is no learning, there is no positive attitude, there are no agreements, there is no organization, the strength or weakness of a company relies heavily on its leaders in key positions.

Planning:

It is necessary at all times to know where we are going, what time we need to get there and how we will use that time to make the most of it.

Organization:
It is the way it is divided into tasks according to the skills, knowledge and experience of each team member, so that each one takes advantage of their abilities and performs the tasks more efficiently, in the times and forms established in planning.

Communication:

The way to know that we are all going towards the same goal, is to communicate to everyone, about everything that happens good and bad, express opinions or suggestions to improve or correct something, but never remain silent.

All companies are different and each one works differently, it is the diversity that exists in the world to create a positive organizational culture.

The important thing is that each entrepreneur finds what best suits their business philosophy idea, but understanding that depending on the one they choose, it will have a negative or positive impact on the work environment and, of course, on productivity and level of worker satisfaction.

Organization and Structure

Organization:

An organization is made up of the elements that a company uses to be functional, such as processes, policies, facilities, work plans, areas and their defined functions, information flows, positions and profiles, training plans and development etc.

The organization levels are to identify the different responsibilities and roles among the people who work in the company.

It begins by defining the managers, who are the people in charge of making the critical decisions of the company, who will analyze each situation that may affect the interests and direction of the company, as well as detect growth opportunities and take advantage of them in the best possible way. In this way, they will be responsible for guiding the entire work team towards the same path.

Then at the management levels, who will receive the indications about the new decisions and who will be responsible for planning the most efficient way of doing the activities that shape the new decisions and achieve the objectives requested by the managers.

Finally, employees are responsible for executing tasks.

Executive level - Their influence on the work environment will be with the kind of decisions that are made, not only thinking about the benefit of the company, but also the benefit of the workers, therefore if the employees are not motivated, they will not execute decisions as expected and the objective will not be achieved, the way they communicate the indications to the lower levels will be fundamental not only for a good understanding of the ideas but also to achieve the required impact of conscience.

Management Level - Their influence on the work environment is very important as they are the link between managers and workers at the operational level, they are the ones who receive instructions about new decisions and are the ones who organize people to carry out activities. For this reason, they must take special care in the attitude they will have with their collaborators with intelligent leadership.

He must show authority when necessary, but always with respect, when planning, he must show sufficient ability to make his collaborators work in the activities for which they have the greatest qualities and thus take advantage of the full potential of each one, distributing work equally and do it at the planned times, with sufficient mental and emotional balance to maintain good control while maintaining harmony.

Employees - Their influence on the work climate will be first to create in themselves the awareness of doing their job well, with commitment and maximum effort, maintaining the mental and emotional balance for a good work relationship with confidence and collaboration with all their colleagues. with your boss and with the executives, that allow you to work synergistically, so that the work flows and the objectives of the company are achieved.

If you manage to establish culture of change strategies and they are done at all levels, you will have a positive impact on the work environment, since each person, from the development of their own activities, will contribute to building an environment of harmony and respect, which although they will not be exempt from conflicts arising, because it is part of the daily coexistence in a company for several hours a day, the resolution of conflicts will be easier because everyone will have the same will to solve them by contributing ideas and solutions.

Structure
The structure is made up of two factors:

The non-palpable one where the company's philosophy is taken into consideration and in the way it is transmitted to the workers through the Mission, Vision, Values and Objectives both individually and in common with the company.

The palpable one, in which the real estate, the facilities, office equipment, furniture and everything necessary for the performance of the activities are taken into account.

A company must cement its structure with firm foundations not only in infrastructure, that is, the physical part, but also the logical and emotional part that will govern the behavior of the people who work in it, to build a positive work climate.

Congruence

Congruence refers to the way in which the company behaves with integrity and values in relation to the structure with which it intends to operate and face the challenges to achieve the expected success and also refers to choosing the ideal people to achieve it.

Most companies are more concerned with creating job profiles with more focus on knowledge and experience and less or nothing on the emotional, mental and attitude side.

And why focus more on a mental and emotional profile? The reason is very simple, it is much easier to teach those who lack knowledge, than to try to change the bad attitude and mental and emotional conflicts in an adult person.

For this reason, I propose to break paradigms and give equal importance to mental and emotional balance, and create job profiles according to the Mission, Vision, Philosophy and values not only to knowledge and experience, the result would be more favorable, because the The company will recruit the right people to build and maintain a positive work climate.

In human relationships, conflicts arise at any time, but if you have people who are mentally and emotionally prepared and willing to resolve conflicts, they will be able to create and maintain a positive work environment (because they were selected from the start), resolution will be easier of conflicts, and of course they will be people who will learn faster to do their job better.

In human relations, as we all know, conflicts arise at any time, but if you have people who are mentally and emotionally prepared and willing to create and maintain a positive work environment, (because they were selected from the beginning), it will be easier to conflict resolution, and of course they will be people who will learn faster to do their job better.

"Don't recruit geniuses who hate your life, better recruit people happy with your life and turn them into geniuses."

It is a measure that must be taken into account from the beginning, because the consequence of not doing it can get out of control, and you will have to fire people who should never have been recruited and have to carry out a restructuring that costs a lot of money and in time, with very hurt relationships and legal conflicts that will last a long time.

All of this can be avoided by doing a good recruiting and recruiting job with a different idea.

Mission

We all know that the Company's Mission is the reason for existing, but it also tries to explain the way in which the service offered or the product that is manufactured is provided to cover a need, therefore the psychological profile must be very clear and emotional of the people more than by the experience, it will be able to fulfill that mission.

And that is accomplished by creating suitable job profiles and descriptions and a recruitment and selection process choosing the best candidates who are closest to the Mission.

If the Mission is more focused on the development of technology or the manufacture of a product, the correct approach would be to attract talent with more creative qualities and with a great capacity for analysis.

These concepts may seem obvious, but on many occasions I have observed people in a job who, when analyzing it, observed that the mission of the company, or the job description, or the profile of the worker, were not related to each other , and is it wrong or not?

Vision

The Company's Vision should be a well-defined long-term goal, but it can only be reached if employees also believe in it and are trained, motivated and committed.

In the same way, the job description, the profile and the Vision must be consistent, since it will be easier to work with people who want to do their best and help the company to fulfill the Vision, than to work with people who must be forced for them to do their job and take longer to fulfill the Vision or even never fulfill it.

Philosophy

It is the idea of the way in which the company will operate within, the way of interacting among the people who work in it.

The philosophy is linked to the mindset of each entrepreneur who decides to create a source of income but at the same time, also creates a source of work for other people, so if the philosophy is based only on earning a lot of money, he will achieve it but with a negative work climate, with frustration of the workers, because the only thing that will matter will be money and not people.

On the other hand, if the philosophy is based on promoting the development of people and creating a positive work environment for them, in other words, the most important thing is people first, this will happen: Happy workers, work harder and better.

The key to achieving expected success is finding the perfect balance so that profits and people are equally important.

Each entrepreneur and managers who run a company have to choose the philosophy to achieve the expected success of their companies.

I believe that the success of a company could be based on these basic principles:

- You must meet a social need
- You must respect the environment
- Must generate decent employment
- The company must grow and make its workers grow
- Must generate profits and pay taxes
- Must provide a benefit to the owner
- Must provide a benefit to suppliers
- Must provide a benefit to customers
- Must bring a benefit to society
- You must bring a benefit to your city
- Must bring a benefit to the countryD and be of benefit to the country

The business philosophy focused on the work environment:

How we want our people to be:

With demotivation:

Strategy: threats, scolding, yelling, humiliation, ridicule, destructive criticism, harassment.

Result: bad work environment, staff turnover, low productivity, short company life time.

With motivation:

Strategies: training, rewards, recognitions, congratulations, respect, pressure of work with criteria.

Result: good work environment, staff stability, high productivity, long life of the company.

How we want our leaders to be:

Overbearing boss:

Strategies he uses: scolds, yells, humiliates, mocks, criticizes, blocks development.

Result: bad work environment, staff turnover, short company life time.

Smart leader:

Strategies you use: teach, reward, recognize, congratulate, respect, drive development.

Result: good work environment, confidence, motivation, commitment, stability of the staff, long life of the company.

Values

Choosing the company's values, or redefining them, should be those that best fit the philosophy and that will directly influence all the labor and commercial relations of the organization.

But, the question is whether entrepreneurs and managers have really stopped to analyze whether the values that they show their clients and employees have the same projection so that they justify their reason for being.

Values should not be just words that adorn a wall, or words that workers must learn by heart but do not put into practice, if in companies values were adopted as a way of coexisting daily for everyone, the company would function better, because the values would be real.

What does a manager look for in an employee?

They are looking for people who are not interested in just having a job and earning money, they are looking for professional people who have goals in their lives and who take their work as a means to contribute something to society, who have the desire to be part of an organization not only As employees, the only thing that worries them is collecting money for their days worked, but as true collaborators, who contribute to strengthening the organization with commitment and constant effort, in short, people willing to "give" and "receive".

Recommendations for managers to achieve a positive work environment

Investment

It is very easy to think that an investment is rather an expense that they try to avoid, to "take care of the company's income" and spend as little as possible, but if this were a correct theory, there would be no successful managers with a broader vision of how to stay on course for their companies, they take care of expenses but they also invest more because they know that they will return in greater quantity.

When I speak of investment, I am referring to everything in which it is necessary to "risk" a little bit of earnings in important aspects of great impact within companies, that is, in people, in human capital, because they are people who They decide to give their time to the company, that every day they leave their families to go to work for several hours and do their job as well as possible, so it is a smart way to invest.

It is worth nothing to have great managers, if you do not have great employees, it is like trying to use a car with an excellent driver as director, but with a broken engine, it means that we have someone to drive (managers), but the engine that makes walk, (employees) cannot do it well, the only way to move it is to push it, just like a poorly managed company with poor human capital.

The solution is very simple, repair the engine and if possible make it more powerful, some suggestions to invest could be:

- Invest in better facilities and work equipment
- Invest in listening to their needs and let them participate and make proposals for solutions to conflicts
- Invest in giving them more of a person with interests and needs and less of an employee with obligations
- Invest in providing them the possibility of developing and growing within the company with constant training programs, life plans, succession and replacement plans

The return on that great investment will be with committed and motivated employees who will help the company with greater productivity, an excellent work environment, high quality work, goal fulfillment, sustained growth and obviously higher profits.

Other recommendations:

- Employees are not enemies, they are people with feelings and needs that need the help of the company, they are very important, not to forget that they are the engine of the company.

- Currently, it is no longer useful to give workers the responsibility to rate what is going wrong in the company with work climate surveys that never give the expected results, the manager must know what is wrong, be more self-critical, you just have to act with judgment and vision.

- Make decisions about the direction of the company with a sense of social responsibility, never think that the company's interests are the only thing that matters, those who have thought so, today have only a memory of their companies, decisions are made considering all aspects that influence the company's development and future, money, objects, but, above all, people.

- The saying "win, win" is a great truth, if the workers are given little, the company will receive little from them, if the workers receive more, the company will get a lot from them.

It is possible to think that it is risky because some people do not value, abuse and unfortunately it is also true, but remember what we talked about in the previous chapter, the type of people who will be recruited, consenting people, not abusive.

A good work environment starts from a polite greeting or a friendly facial expression, everyone should show education and respect towards others, even if they do not have an important position.

Whoever thinks so, proves to be insecure, because these people believe that a high-level position is what makes them important, but it is not so, we are important because of what we are internally and how we behave.

"There are no people in the world more valuable than others, only people with a selfish soul and a mistaken belief."

What is a employee looking for in a company?

People look for a job to meet different needs and not just compensation in money for their work, the point is to know how far the company is willing to take these aspects into account with its staff, understanding that they must be the main element of an organization whose purpose is sustained growth and the achievement of objectives, since they are crucial aspects for a positive work climate.

Stability:
It is the need to stay in a place that gives you peace of mind and security for the future, to make short and long-term plans, both personally and professionally.

Acceptance:
It is the need for a person to integrate into a social and work environment, in which he can create bonds of trust with colleagues and friends.

Recognition:
It is the need to maintain high self-esteem and self-confidence, for the achievement of objectives that are publicly recognized.

Success:
It is the need to experience the feeling of accomplishment by overcoming challenges, elevates self-confidence and your image towards others.

Recommendations for employees for a positive work climate

- Analyze your own attitudes before judging those of others.

- The boss does not have to be an enemy, he is a person with many responsibilities and concerns who trusts his team, who needs your help so that together they achieve their objectives.

- If something seems unfair to you, first find out the reasons, if it still seems unfair, propose solutions instead of acting negligently or rebelliously, that attitude not only affects the company, it affects your image as a professional.
- The work environment is generated by everyone, at all levels, starting oneself to do for others, what we hope they do for us.

- If something goes wrong, not looking for culprits, is wasting valuable time and makes you see yourself as someone who does not know how to work in a team, better looks for solutions, providing ideas, we will feel better about ourselves and make a better impression among colleagues.

- Having a real commitment at work, not only taking it as a means of subsistence, the efforts will always be rewarded in some way, because if the company does well, the workers will also do well.

- Managers always try to make the most appropriate decisions for the good of the company, sometimes they may seem unfair, but before judging let's think that they risk a lot of money and prestige so that people have a job, if you still feel that something is not Okay, express it, but with intelligence and respect, if it is reasonable, you will have more possibilities of being heard so you will be part of the solution and not part of the problem.

- Supporting coworkers, developing in ourselves the satisfaction of helping others, makes us bigger as people and the rewards come in many ways.

- Respect the employees' personality, it is impossible for all people to think and act in the same way, it is about developing the ability to adapt to circumstances, always remember that there is no perfect place to work or perfect colleagues or the perfect boss.

- If the company strives to give more to its employees than it is obliged to give for our well-being, we must value it, not make the mistake of abusing those benefits, let's change that culture of waste. Change begins with oneself.

- The company can invest in training and development, but you must understand that it is a shared responsibility, take care of yourself and train yourself as possible, in addition to the training you receive from the company, research, ask, get involved, read books, attend conferences, your development is not only the responsibility of the company, it is also yours.

- Do not demand what you have not earned with results, you should not feel that you deserve it ahead of time, that it is your work, your attitude and achievements that speaks, and thus the possibilities are much greater to obtain what you ask for.

- The boss should not be a target of criticism and sneering, if you think that your boss does not have enough capacity, there are ways to express it, with respect and intelligence, even consider a change of functions, or a change of area or if the situation is difficult to resolve and you think you cannot adapt, so simply change jobs.

Chapter 3

Radical changes

Radical changes are very necessary when you discover that something is wrong and you need to remedy it, or to prevent it from happening.

Also because they are the most reliable way to correct something by ensuring that the change is final.

Over time, I have found that radical changes do not happen for several reasons:

- For not harming someone's interests
- For change's resistance
- Because a lot of money is spent
- Because it requires spending valuable time.

It is important to understand that superficial changes do not solve problems, the reality is that they will still be there causing conflicts.

Therefore, you must detect the problems that can be corrected with a superficial solution that will not cause inconvenience and which problems require a radical change.

To achieve this you must first know what causes a problem and look for smart solutions that cause the least possible negative impact, because there will always be risk when you make important changes to correct problems.

When we finally realize that radical changes are needed in the company to improve the working environment, you should start by deepening the investigation as much as possible to ensure that you can detect possible causes and be willing to take the risks involved in applying the necessary strategies to achieve radical changes.

Now we will analyze the most common problems in most companies and the situations that can be the solution and that require a radical change:

If the problem is an employee

We must find out if ...

- He has a concern or something that bothers him at work in the workplace.
- He has some kind of personal problem that is unrelated to the job that makes him uneasy.
- He has a personal problem with a coworker.
- They have a personal problem with their boss.
- He does not have the necessary profile of the position.
- He has aggressive tendencies.
- He is not very adept at managing his negative emotions
- He has not received regular training in the last 6 months.
- The tools that the company gives him to do his job are not adequate.
- He does not feel recognized, motivated, or listened to.
- He does not make feedback with his boss about his performance
- his salary is lower than in other companies or has few benefits
- The company does not offer you a development plan
- Detects discrimination with him or his coworkers
- There is favoritism on the part of managers
- Bad management of internal communication by the company

If the problem is a boss

We must find out if ...

- He has a concern or something that bothers him at work in the workplace.
- The work load or pressure exceeds its capacity.
- Lacks leadership skills.
- Blocks the development of their subordinates, preventing them from reaching their own level.
- He has a personal problem that makes him uneasy.
- He has a personal problem with a coworker.
- They have a personal problem with their boss
- He does not have the profile of the position that is needed.
- He has not received regular training in the last 6 months.
- The tools the company gives you are not adequate.

If the problem is an executive director

We must find out if...

- He has a concern or something that bothers him at work in the workplace
- Workload or pressure exceeds capacity
- Lacks skills of strategic vision, planning, organization, communication, emotional intelligence
- He blocks the development of his subordinates preventing them from reaching their own level
- He has some kind of personal problem other than work that makes him uneasy
- He has a personal problem with a coworker
- They have a personal problem with their boss
- He does not have the profile of the position that is needed
- He has not received regular training in the last 6 months.
- Analyze his leadership style
- Analyze his communication style
- Analyze his ability to visualize problems and solutions.
- Analyze his ability to lead work teams
- Analyze your behavior with your team

If the problem is a department

We must find out if ...

- You must analyze the profiles of all members
- You must analyze the profile and leadership of the department head.
- you may need to relocate or rotate staff
- You must conduct an individual interview with each member
- Redefine department functions and responsibilities
- You must carry out a study of workloads and the appropriate distribution among the work team
- you must analyze the positions in the organization chart and see if they are correct
- you must Create integration dynamics

If the problem is company-wide

- Redefine the Company's Mission, Vision and Values
- Redefine the company's philosophy
- Perform a 360 ° evaluation among all employees
- Redefine job descriptions and validate with the profiles of current occupants.
- Redesign organization chart of jobs
- Analyze leadership styles of managers
- Compare salaries with other companies
- Redefine benefits scheme
- Promote integration activities such as sports or recreational activities
- Strengthen recognition for achieving objectives with higher impact incentives such as travel, gifts, etc.
- Redefine training programs
- Invest in improving facilities, computer equipment, uniforms, furniture, decoration, lighting, etc.
- Redefine Policies and Procedures
- Redefine communication systems
- Create an area or hire an internal manager to generate Organizational Development strategies
- Request support from experts in Organizational Development consulting

Chapter 4

Change and improvement strategies

Recruitment and staff selection

Build commitment from the start

It is hard to believe, but recruitment and commitment have a very close relationship, but few people have the capacity to understand and apply it.

We all know that the commitment of workers is fundamental to the fulfillment of both individual and company goals, but, how do you manage to develop employee commitment? Most of them expect more from their company than receiving a salary, more than just a job to meet their needs, they need to feel that the company does more to support them in their personal and professional development.

Obtain experience, knowledge and skills, and thus apply the rule of "win, win", because the company wins with a highly committed employee and the employee wins in obtaining the real possibility of developing professionally in their workplace.

Everything is going very well, but unfortunately, very few are the companies that are willing to invest in their human capital, these days companies are looking for people who have already learned everything before, that the investment has been made by another company, but we must be aware that a worker's commitment begins with a company's willingness to invest in its employees.

Recruitment today has become a destructive mechanism of commitments and motivations, because as I said before, companies are looking for people who already know everything, so that they do not have to "spend valuable time" giving them the opportunity to learn in the company, in developing and training them, and that is the reason why employees become unmotivated since they arrive at the company.

Managers simply do not have enough strategic vision to understand it, and that is the first mistake recruiters fail to generate commitment in a new worker, because they are offered work but that is no longer enough, because they are offered little and are it demands a lot.

When a recruiter finally hires an employee who has all the necessary requirements of the job, managers must be aware that it is very likely that as someone who owes the company nothing for its development, will not feel so committed and will probably leave as soon as you have a better offer from another company and won't mind leaving.

What is the fault ?, The company does nothing to generate in it any feeling of commitment for the reason already explained of not wanting to invest time in its development.

Make a good impression from the start

The activity of recruiting staff is nothing more or less the first impression that is created of the company abroad, towards applicants, therefore, from the way of posting a vacancy, you are already sending a message, which can be positive or negative of what the company is like and its philosophy, or, in other words, what a person will find if they are accepted to work in the company.

It is important to understand that you have to be careful in what you want to communicate, because otherwise, all you can do is give a negative message from the company and the candidates may create the wrong idea of what they will find there.

A message that says you don't care about your employees and that you only care about the outcome before people do, need not explain that after a while that will lead to frustrated, discouraged, uncompromising workers and they will be waiting for the first opportunity to leave.

Then the company will have another of the big problems in companies, the constant turnover of personnel and the flight of talent that

It is very expensive, because other companies take advantage of them.

And of course it will be a good reason for a candidate to lose interest in participating in the recruitment process and much less for working in the company, and as a consequence, several talents will be constantly lost without having known them, than other companies with a different vision. if they will take advantage.

Leaders from the start

The people that the company recruits to be bosses are also those who are most affected by the positive or negative work environment, since a large part of the responsibility falls on them to improve and maintain a good work environment.

For this reason, hiring bosses with features of violence and aggressiveness, believing that it is what the company needs to "force" employees to work, because those are "bosses with character", is one of the biggest mistakes of executives and perhaps without thinking about it, they are already dedicating their company to suffer a totally negative work climate.

When hiring people to fill positions of high importance, more weight is given to experience and knowledge and less to the profile that is consistent with the Mission, Vision, Values and Philosophy.

Knowledge and experience are acquired, but values and integrity develop from childhood, we all know that as an adult it is very difficult to develop them, people with the right profile will guarantee the expected success and achievement of all objectives at the same time. They receive support in their personal and professional development, creating with this greater commitment from people and with much less problems for the company.

Identify people with leadership, who help a favorable work climate, remember that the positive or negative work climate begins to form from the recruitment of the right people.

"Don't Hire" Bosses With Character "That Treat Workers Badly, Better Hire Smart Leaders" That Help Them Work Better.

Instinct, intuition and seeing beyond the obvious

Recruitment is the art of knowing how to identify talents and abilities in people that match what a company needs to perform specific functions.

But it is not an easy task, there is no defined way to carry out the recruitment, each recruiter does it differently, but the most important thing is to never neglect some aspects that help to choose better, since it is necessary to further develop instinct, intuition and ability to see beyond what is evident in a person.

We know that not all people are the right ones for all companies, but relying solely on finding people who have all the requirements to be possible candidates is a mistake, because intuition is very important when selecting a candidate to do a job.

Intuition gives the necessary sensitivity to be able to detect talents and abilities in a person, even if they do not have all the requirements, since, based only on selecting candidates with this sole criterion, the company loses the opportunity to attract true talents, which can be become the best employees or bosses.

By this I mean that the ability to see beyond what is evident in the candidates, will help to analyze more deeply a person, who has the most important requirements and trust him to support him in developing the requirements of the position that he does not have. they are less important when you have already been hired.

It seems risky and in fact it is, but in any case there are risks when hiring a candidate that you think is the right one, and then it turns out that he is the right candidate, so the risk is one way or another.

Trust will generate a feeling of gratitude in the employee that will become commitment and loyalty to the company, because they will not have the opportunity to have a job, and the company offers them the opportunity to develop from the moment they start their employment relationship.

That is something that almost no company dares to do, and think that from that moment you will have a motivated and committed employee who will not only strive to do their job well, it will also be a generator of a positive work climate.

Everyone is free to choose the way to recruit, the traditional way of choosing the candidate who already knows everything and rejecting a talented candidate and taking the risk of trusting them, developing them within the company to create a true commitment in him.

Aspects to evaluate:

According to my experience, generally in recruitment, three main aspects are basically evaluated:

Intellectual
Where IQ, knowledge, skills, competencies, techniques and experience are evaluated.

Mental
Where the candidate's concepts about teamwork, communication, integration, interpersonal relationships, leadership, work culture, values, respect are evaluated.

Emotional
Where the psychological and emotional situation of the candidate is evaluated, if he has resentments, frustrations, complexes, envies, personality traits and everything that may affect his emotional balance and his job performance and integration into a work team.

The key is to find a balance in the 3 elements when defining the profiles of each position and what type of people may be hired to occupy each position, taking care that they are most consistent with the Mission, Vision, Values and Philosophy of That way you create the right combination of structure and human capital.

If you give more importance to the intellectual factor, the type of candidate could be rather a cold and calculating person, with more attitude of strict boss and not of training leader, the result will be the most important thing for him, it is very likely to generate tension in your work team, with little probability of being an change agent and influencing other people to improve and maintain a good work environment.

On the other hand, if you give more importance to the mental and emotional factor but in a positive sense, you could be a candidate with great communication and leadership skills to lead work teams, you will have a more open attitude to support people to develop professionally and of course, being an change agent to create a favorable work environment.

If the emotional factor is given more importance even in a positive sense, it is not recommended, because to direct a group of people an emotional balance is not enough because at any time it can be broken, it is necessary to have a combination of all the elements, because you can run the risk of hiring a person with great possibilities of becoming a negative leader, capable of generating only a negative work climate.

There are techniques that have been developed to achieve these changes, such as the Assessment Center technique, to assess how the candidate reacts in a situation similar to reality, in addition to the interview and the psychometric evaluation, to have a broader parameter on the conditions of each candidate and assessing them more accurately is a true test of talent.

"The talents that some waste, others take advantage of."

The polls

In my experience of having applied and answered many surveys of work environment in companies, I have seen that the objective is at odds with the strategy, I explain it as follows:

Problem: Nonconformity of the staff
Objective: Obtain information
Strategy: Staff survey
Risk: Little truth in the answers
Result: Unreliable information to make sound decisions

Employees' feeling of not being heard.

If you analyze the real results obtained from applying a survey, you conclude that it is a strategy that reveals very little of what you want to know, let's start by understanding that applying a workplace climate survey can be for two reasons, to prevent possible problems or to correct when the problem is already evident.

In both cases, it inevitably falls into a game of anonymous questions and answers and it is not objective, you create a great barrier of trust and communication, the message to employees is that to express their feelings and opinions, the company is not interested in listening or to dialogue and nothing will change.

A manager knows very well what is right and what is wrong within a company, for that reason, I think that it is not even necessary to apply a work climate survey to know what is wrong, for example if the company decides to pay a low salary at its workers and also hires bad bosses who mistreat their employees with threats and yelling, it is absurd to apply a workplace climate survey of employees' relationship with their bosses, because the answers are obvious.

This discourages employees, because surveys with targeted questions always end in charts for executives, and employees know perfectly well that their true opinions were not heard.

It is time to break with some paradigms and communication barriers that instead of improving the work environment, make it worse. So dare to try new ways to communicate with employees and know exactly what is wrong and what is right, so you can get employees to express what they really feel and think without fear.

It will always be better for them to feel the confidence to do so because, in addition to being able to express their feelings, employees and executives also commit to doing what is necessary to change what needs to be changed.

New survey approach

New survey idea

The idea is with a survey more attached to the spontaneous and everyday situations that arise daily and directly affect the working environment and achieve greater awareness and sincerity in the intended result.

The idea is to have the same objective of obtaining information and knowing the opinion of the employees, but with a different strategy, in a more open way and in an environment of trust.

To achieve this, I propose to use a technique that I have developed and is called - "DxD Technique" - and it consists of the following:

It is done in 5 stages, every day.

First stage:

Each employee records in a notebook all the situations they experience in a bad and good work day, for two weeks, they must be explained as much as possible, then they will write 3 possible causes that the worker considers have caused a bad result or a good result, one The answer must refer to your boss, the other answer to your colleagues and the other answer to yourself.

In this way you can measure more real and reliable what the employee feels at work and discover what needs to be changed and better decisions can be made to solve problems.

at the end of the exercise, in the last column, the employee will write the correction or solution that he proposes so that the negative situation becomes positive and the positive situation remains positive.

The objective of this technique is that the employee does not answer what the manager wants, but rather records real positive and negative situations of what he lives daily with his bosses, coworkers and executives, he points out the possible causes openly without the condition of directed responses as in a survey and most importantly, it allows you the freedom to think and propose solutions at the moment and in a practical way.

With this it is achieved that the employee feels listened to and with the possibility of participating in the decisions to improve what has to be improved, exercise is a more reliable parameter of the work climate in the company when applying it and making decisions and actions more accurate.

Second stage:

Over the next two weeks, employees implement the corrections they have proposed.

Third stage:

Employees analyze their records and generate a list of conclusions about what they were able to correct and how it was accomplished. What they could not correct and why.

Fourth stage:

Hold a meeting of each area and each employee and managers will present their conclusions so that everyone knows the results. A Human Resources representative must be present to generate agreements, solutions and actions and make a work plan to achieve the necessary change or changes and thus to improve the work environment.

And finally, in the fifth stage, an evaluation of the result is carried out to measure the scope of achieving the objective.

The objective of each stage is:

1st. Stage: Identify
2nd. Stage: Act
3rd. Stage: Diagnose
4th. Stage: Solve
5th. Stage: Evaluate

Group dynamics

Dynamics 1 - Fictional role change

The boss poses a problem to the employee and he must analyze it and propose at least two possible solutions, he is asked to take into account that the solution should cause the least possible negative impact to both the employees' interests and those of the company.

Then the same problem is posed to the employee, but with some differences, and the employee must re-analyze the problem and propose a solution.

Finally, the boss and the employee analyze the proposals and the boss gives the feedback indicating if their proposals are viable or not and why.

This dynamic has several very useful purposes, that the employee sees the complexity of his boss to face problems and find solutions and that this generates more awareness when judging his colleagues, his boss or managers.

Another purpose is to allow workers to show their creative talent and analytical capacity to solve problems, to better understand the strengths and weaknesses of human capital, and to be able to generate a development plan. Another purpose is that the boss has the opportunity to know new approaches or ways of seeing a problem.

Another way of doing this dynamic is the opposite way, that is, the boss is faced with problems that may be presented to an employee to do his job, and the boss analyzes the situations and carries out the same activity as in the first case.

Here the purpose is that the boss knows the problems that an employee has to carry out his work and better understand the cause of the problems, the boss, the worker, or the managers, or if it is of a labor or personal type, training, planning or communication, etc.

Dynamics 2 - Approach

The employee spends a few hours in his boss's office to see what a work day is like for him, and all the situations that must be resolved.

Then the opposite is done, the boss spends a few hours in the employee's place observing what his work day is like and all the situations that he must resolve.

This dynamic may be difficult to carry out due to confidential information, however, it is worth thinking about the possibility of carrying it out perhaps with some adjustments to critical information, but this activity is an effective strategy to shake the conscience of the boss and the manager. employee, to understand situations that normally in a common work day, it would not be possible to experience and to sensitize.

Efectividad

To help employees become more efficient, a simple support plan can be implemented to plan and execute their daily tasks more efficiently, this will bring, as a benefit, the development of skills and benefit for the company by having more efficient people than increase productivity.

In the following model, it is shown how employees can be classified according to their activities planning and execution skills, and detect the weak points that must be reinforced to reach the highest point of the classification, which is the letter " A".

It is important to mention that, if you detect people at the lowest level that is the letter "D", it would be reasonable to think that he is not a correct person for the position to which he was hired.

In this situation, there are three possibilities, the first is to fire him, the second is to evaluate him to detect other skills and see the possibility of relocating him to another position, and the third is to train him and gradually move each level up to level "A", but That will depend on the philosophy that prevails in each company to make the decision.

For employees who are at level "B" and "C", the recommendation is to train them to gradually level up to level "A", but it is important to mention that it is not good to jump levels, that is, jump from level "C" to level "A" directly because he probably will not succeed and he and his boss are frustrated and a climate of tension and mistrust will be generated, it is better to make them go first to level "B" and once Achieve and feel safe, start your training towards level "A".

Effectiveness Diagnostic Model
Ricardo Pérez P.

Efficient

- **A** — Plan and execute
  - Low stress
  - Low frustration
  - Less prone to error
  - Little variation of the work plan
  - Achievement of objectives in time

- **B** — Run while planning
  - High stress
  - Low frustration
  - More prone to error
  - Much variation of the work plan
  - Achievement of objectives with little delay

Inefficient

- **C** — Run without planning
  - High stress
  - High frustration
  - High probability of error
  - There is no work plan
  - Achievement of objectives with a long delay

- **D** — Doesn't plan and execute poorly
  - High stress
  - High frustration
  - Blunt errors
  - There is no work plan
  - No goal achievement

Training process

An easy way to plan

Planning activities is the safest way to manage time and make the most of it, it is a way to start developing skills to reach the highest point and be an efficient worker at work.

Planning should be a daily habit, in order to ensure the achievement of short and long-term goals.

The following example explains how you can do a simple and easy to understand planning to learn how to plan, it is a simple table with columns and lines where the task is written and all the conditions are completed.

The last column is the most important because it is the deadline to finish the task, it is the one that serves as an indicator to know if it is possible to maintain a regularity in the habit of finishing what begins, to the extent that the person disciplines himself in accomplishing With your own set times, you will notice how it gradually reaches a satisfactory level of effectiveness, but it will be necessary to use this method until it becomes a habit and you no longer need to use the method manually.

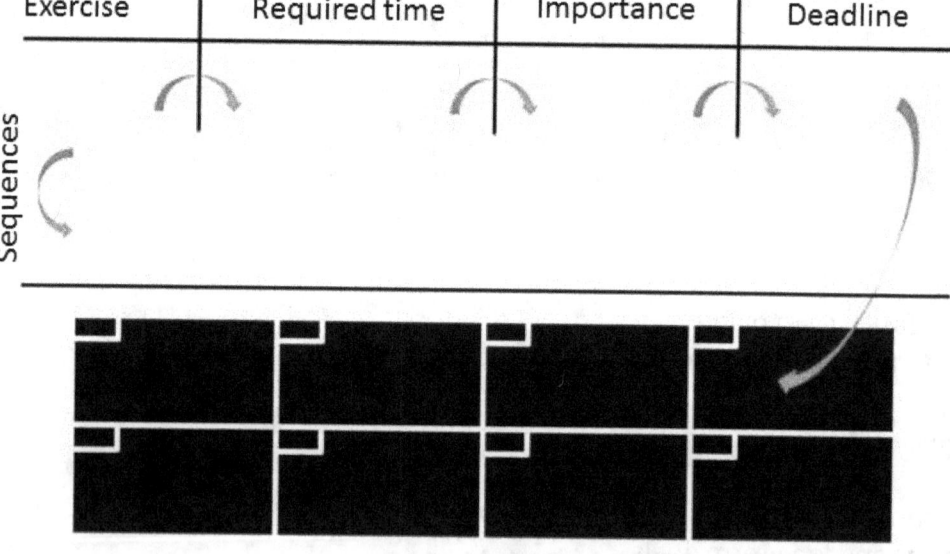

How to plan

Additional - costs, managers, documents, etc.

Work with daily goals

For employees who are not used to working for goals, it can help to use a method to force themselves to meet goals per day, it is necessary to create a blog where every day before starting the work day, the tasks that are recorded They can be completed in one day, they are recorded as goals that at the end of the day must be met.

The employee will be able to evaluate himself or his boss, either weekly or monthly, generating statistics that serve as indicators to measure productivity and work efficiency, if the indicator shows more goals not met, it is necessary to do an in-depth analysis among several factors such as:

- The distribution of work activities
- Lack of planning
- Employee profile must match job description
- Quality in communication and distribution tasks
- Quality in the interrelation between boss and employee

All are aspects to take care of that can harm a favorable work environment and support productivity.

Reinforcement cycles

It is what all companies must do constantly, repeating over and over so that employees do not become discouraged and there is a situation of bad work climate, staff turnover, low productivity and everything that may affect productivity.

Just as our bodies require food from time to time to function properly, companies require to "feed" their personnel in various ways to function properly.

Reinforcement cycles help keep the company running optimally, because if these cycles are only performed once they lose strength, ideally they should be cycles that never stop.

Reinforcement Cycles
Ricardo Pérez P.

	businessmen			employees	
Need →	$ ←	income	→	$	
Solution →	company ←	medium	→	Job	
	- Contract - Benefits			Security	
REINFORCEMENT (CYCLES)	- Sense of belonging - Participation, proposals - Positive work environment			Commitment	WORK CYCLES
	- Leadership (bosses) - Feedback - Fair salary and incentives - Flexible schedules			Motivation	
	- Sufficient and adequate tools - Constant training - Orientation, advice (mentors)			Goals	
	- recognition			Results	
	- Career plan - Personal development - Promotion to better positions			Stability	
Target →		Stable company in constant growth			

This means:

- If the employee feels safe, he will be committed
- If the employee feels committed, he will be motivated
- If the employee feels motivated, he will achieve goals
- If the employee achieves objectives, he will achieve the result
- If you achieve the result, you will achieve stability in your position
- If you achieve stability, you will achieve growth

Now we will analyze each point to understand the concept and some useful suggestions:

Sense of belonging:

Company managers need to generate this feeling in their employees to generate more commitment.

Some suggestions may be:

- Badge with the company logo and photograph.
- Company email.
- his name in the company's electronic directory.
- T-shirt or jacket with the company logo.
- Base stationery sign with his name and company logo.
- Door sign with your name and company logo.
- Publication of a yearbook with photographs and stories of all staff.
- Conduct competitions where all workers participate and publish the winners.
- Participate in sports competitions representing the company.
- Provide stationery and mugs with the worker's name and company logo.

Participation:

Encouraging the participation of the workers, makes them feel important and that you listen to their proposals, that they participate in some decisions in the company creates a great sense of commitment.

Some suggestions may be:

- Ask you to come up with proposals to do your job better

Activity proposals for staff integration.

- Competitions

- Permanent program with a communication channel for staff to go to the Human Resources area to express their complaints or suggestions in a respectful way.

- Hold informal meetings at least once a week to find out their opinion about the work environment and listen to employees, so that they can express their doubts and proposals, as well as brainstorm on any issue that could become a issue.

Integration:

Some suggestions may be:

Open day

At least one day a week, managers meet to spend time with employees, this helps to build trust.

It can be at lunchtime, safety committees, sports activities, activities such as chess tournaments, a picnic, courses, etc.

Leadership (bosses):

Motivation must be reinforced every day because it is what helps to achieve the objectives, in this case the behavior of the bosses is very important because they have the responsibility to achieve good communication and a positive attitude with the employees.

Some suggestions may be:

- Develop emotional intelligence for coexistence (the boss must not compel, he must know how to convince).

- High disposition to teamwork (the boss should not be just an observer, he should set the example to work).

- Leader attitude that develops other leaders (you must support the growth of your team, not stagnate them).

Feedback:

It is necessary to help the growth of employees, because they learn to detect their weaknesses and establish forms of continuous improvement.

Some suggestions may be:

- Strengthen bonds of trust between the boss and his staff.
- Open and honest communication between the boss and his staff.
- High willingness to accept mistakes and correct them from managers, bosses and employees.

Incentives:

All people require an incentive that motivates them to achieve what is expected of them, incentives can be in several ways, the most important thing is that the employee receives a reward for their effort.

Some suggestions may be:

- Cash rewards
- Travels
- Days off
- Small gifts

Competition:

It is the way to motivate each employee to strive, to encourage fair competition in which all employees have the same opportunity to show their qualities to better perform the job, it focuses on developing and detecting leadership skills in employees and training better workers personally and professionally.

Some suggestions may be:

- Create projects and form work teams to detect positive leaders among the members
- Ask employees to contribute project ideas

Tools:

The company must provide employees with everything necessary to do their job well

Some suggestions may be:

- Suitable computer and accessories
- Desk and comfortable chair in good condition
- Furniture for storing documents (filing cabinet)
- Good lighting
- Stationery shop articles
- Copier
- Uniforms (depending if the activity requires it)

Training:

If the company invests in the training of its employees, it will obtain as a benefit a job of better quality and in less time, which means an investment with a safe return and that at the same time will lead to savings, in conclusion, it is a mutual benefit.

Some suggestions may be:

- Training courses paid by the company
- Financial support for Master's degrees for employees
- Create a training department with trained personnel to deliver training courses on various subjects themselves and to get the best courses at the best prices from training companies.

Orientation:

Support for workers must be, in many ways, advising them on different topics, whether personal or work, for their professional and personal growth.

Some suggestions may be:

- Offer permanent psychological attention service.
- Ease for the employee seeking professional attention, but paid by the company.

Recognition:

Achieving goals is something that causes great satisfaction to employees and is an excellent opportunity to recognize the effort.

Some suggestions may be:

- Place a blackboard in full view of the objective achieved, the impact achieved, and the people who participated.

- Written recognition in the form of a diploma delivered by managers personally.

- Electronic newsletter informing the entire company of achievements obtained by a department or an employee.

Acknowledgments

Individual awards

Recognition is an appropriate way of letting an employee know that he has accomplished his job, exceeding expectations, and the company shows his appreciation for the positive impact his effort caused, whether with public recognition or any Another way.

For example: In a company with 500 employees, if only one person is recognized, the employee will know that he has little chance of winning and that can discourage him from competing, it is better to create recognitions by department, and thus each worker will have more possibilities of Winning and being recognized will be more prizes, but everyone will also be more motivated.

Let's change the corporate culture and adopt new customs to motivate employees.

Business policies

When it comes to making policies so that everyone behaves the same way and knows what is right to do and what is not right to do, it is a common mistake to ban everything that is possible, thinking that this will better protect the interests of the company and In part it is correct to do so, but be careful, remember that from there a bad work climate could already be generated.

For this reason, what would it be like to think about making policies in a positive sense, to motivate people to respect policies instead of using them to threaten and punish.

Communication policies

Communication policies are very important for the correct use of resources and responsible management of the information that flows daily in an organization.

Poor communication can lead to costly mistakes, peer conflicts, loss of confidence and many more problems, which can have a very negative impact on the work environment.

Communicating to us can only be in three forms, oral, printed or electronic, therefore, you should be aware of how you use resources and which element works best for each situation.

Chapter 5

Change measurement indicators

To know the result of the strategies used and measure the magnitude of the changes achieved, you can use indicators that show a starting point and the end point to determine if the objective was achieved or not, as well as progress meters between one point and another, This will help us to design new strategies to continue the process of the desired change.

Before designing and implementing the indicators, you must pay attention to some factors that will serve to structure the format of each indicator well for each situation.

For example, if you need to measure staff turnover, you should not only use the total number of workers and the total number of casualties in a given time to know the percentage of turnover, in addition to that, you can complement the information taking into account elements such as:

- The dates of greatest losses
- The most frequent causes
- The areas with the most rotation

I suggest that before starting to implement improvement strategies, start with managers making a consensus involving all employees at any level, so that each one makes a list of situations that they consider adverse, both those that are directly related to their activity and those that are not related, that list should contain everything that each one of them detects that they are doing it wrong, or what does not work as a strategy for a good working environment, this will serve to have a broader picture of the problem and to be able to measure in the end, the scope of change's goals.

Indicator suggestions:

- Design indicators to generate daily, weekly and monthly information, in aspects such as: production, sales, market opening, customer response, customer service, satisfaction levels, staff turnover, job demands, reduction of conflicts, achievement of objectives, etc.

- Request the participation of all staff, to express their opinion about changes perceived orally or in writing

- Reapply the DxD assessment and analyze the differences

- Application of a 360° survey

- Customer service quality survey

The results obtained after implementing these indicators must be analyzed very carefully to avoid making hasty decisions that lead to greater problems, and then all the improvement work will be useless.

In this case, a new planning is required on the actions to follow and the time in which they will be implemented, because it will largely depend on the positive or negative reactions of the staff and the impact on the work environment.

In closing, I want to share:

The 10 keys to work environment

THE 10 KEYS TO WORK ENVIRONMENT

1. Don't envy your coworkers
2. Don't feel more important than your coworkers
3. Don't feel smarter than your coworkers
4. Don't blame others for your mistakes
5. Share your knowledge
6. Treat everyone with respect and how you want to be treated
7. Communicate what is positive, avoid intrigue
8. Do not criticize without knowing, better propose solutions
9. Strive first, then demand. Not the other way around
10. Always give a smile and a greeting to your coworkers

If all are based on these keys, it will surely create and maintain a good working environment in our workplace.

It has been a pleasure for me to share this exciting topic with you, I wish that it has contributed something to your lives.

I think we all have the valuable opportunity to change something, to change as people, as professionals, to change the work environment, to change our city, to change our country and then... Why not? ... someday change the world.

Until forever!

Ricardo Pérez P.

ricpez@gmail.com

www.ricardopp.com

www.ingramcontent.com/pod-product-compliance
Lightning Source LLC
Chambersburg PA
CBHW070255220526
45465CB00004B/1632